4 INGREDIENT COOKBOOK

150 Quick & Easy Timesaving Recipes

Bonnie Scott

BONNIE SCOTT

Copyright © 2014 Bonnie Scott

All rights reserved.

Graphics by Cheryl Seslar

ISBN-13: 978-1503239210

CONTENTS

BREADSTICK PRETZELS	11
CRUNCHY PEANUT BUTTER	12
MICROWAVE BUTTER CRUNCH	13
ONE-MINUTE SALSA	14
PITA CHIPS	15
SPICY CROCKPOT PEANUTS	16
FRUIT DIP	17
PINA COLADA FRUIT DIP	18
ONION DIP	19
TACO DIP	20
OKLAHOMA CHILI DIP	21
CHINESE CHICKEN WINGS	22
EASY CHEESE BALL	23
BUTTER MUSHROOMS	24
TIPSY CHICKEN WINGS	25
BUFFALO CHICKEN DIP	26
CRISP TORTILLA CHIPS	27
SWEET N' SOUR WINGS	28

BREAD AND ROLLS 30

CHEDDAR CHEESE PUFFS	30
LITTLE OLIVE TOASTS	31
PEPPERONI BISCUITS	32
TWO CHEESE BREAD	33
PESTO CHEESE LOAF	34
ITALIAN MUFFINS	35
HAWAIIAN CRESCENTS	36
EGG AND CHEESE BREAKFAST BURRITO	37

MAIN DISHES - PORK 40

BONELESS PORK CHOPS	40
HAM POTATO CASSEROLE	41
SLOW COOKER BARBECUED PORK	42
MUSTARD PORK CHOPS	43

PORK AND POTATO BAKE	44
SLOW COOKER BEER CHOPS	45
HAM AND BEANS	46

MAIN DISHES – BEEF 48

MAGIC MEATBALLS	48
VIENNESE STEAK	49
EASY CHILI CASSEROLE	50
STEAK BAKE	51
GOULASH	52
SLOW COOKER BURGUNDY BEEF	53

MAIN DISHES - FISH 55

CORN AND PINEAPPLE SALSA	55
FISH TACOS	56
BAKED COD WITH SOUR CREAM	58
SALMON PATTIES	59
FISH FILLETS WITH TOMATO RICE	60
BROILED FISH WITH DIJON SAUCE	61
SCALLOPS PORTUGUESE	62
FRIED SCALLOPS	63
BROILED FISH FILLETS AND FISH STEAKS	64
CLAM MUSHROOM CASSEROLE	65
FISH-N-CHIPS CASSEROLE	66
GRILLED BOURBON HONEY SALMON	67
BROILED OYSTERS	68
TUNA WITH CAPERS AND LEMON JUICE	69
HALIBUT STEAKS BAKED IN CREAM	70

MAIN DISHES - CHICKEN 72

CHICKEN WITH HERB BUTTER	72
CRANBERRY CHICKEN	73
CHIPOTLE GRILLED CHICKEN	74
CHICKEN BREASTS WITH BACON	75
MICROWAVE BAKED CHICKEN	76

BAKED CHICKEN AND RICE CASSEROLE 77
IRISH CHICKEN 78
CHICKEN MOZZARELLA 79
LEMON CHICKEN 80
PEPSI CHICKEN 81
CHICKEN PARMESAN 82
QUICK CHICKEN GOULASH 83
SUNNY DAY GRILLED CHICKEN 84
SALSA CHICKEN 85
CROCKPOT STROGANOFF 86
LOW-CALORIE JUICY CHICKEN 87
CHICKEN SPAGHETTI 88
CHICKEN BITES 89
BROILED CHICKEN 90
CHICKEN TACOS 91
POLLO ASADO (ROAST CHICKEN) 92
MEXICALI CHICKEN 93
VANILLA AND TARRAGON BAKED CHICKEN 94
BROILED CHICKEN 95
CROCK POT CHICKEN 96
BRILLIANT CHICKEN 97
CHICKEN CASSEROLE 98
ASPARAGUS CHICKEN DELUXE 99
EASY OVEN DINNER 100
SKILLET CHICKEN BREASTS 101
CHICKEN NUGGETS 102
GRILLED HERB-MUSTARD CHICKEN 103
CHICKEN BREASTS WITH MUSHROOMS 104
BAKED CHICKEN 105
HONEY 'N SPICE CHICKEN 106
CHICKEN CACCIATORE 107
CHICKEN FAJITAS 108

SALADS 110

BUTTERMILK SALAD 110
SNICKERS SALAD 111
TOMATO AND CORN SALAD 112
CREAMY CUCUMBERS 113

PISTACHIO SALAD	114
PINK FLUFF	115
TUNA SALAD	116
RED CINNAMON APPLE SALAD	117

SIDE DISHES 119

TWICE-BAKED POTATOES	119
GREEN BEANS AND SALSA	120
ZESTY RED POTATOES	121
SIMPLE MACARONI AND CHEESE	122
POPPY-SEED BOWTIE PASTA	123
GLAZED BABY CARROTS	124
AU GRATIN POTATOES	125
	126
CRAN-APPLE SAUCE	126
WATER CHESTNUTS AND PEAS	127
MICROWAVE CORN ON THE COB	128
FRIED MACARONI	129
JALAPENO CROCKPOT CORN	130
	131
BAKED FRIES	131
CHEESY BROCCOLI AND CHICKEN-TOPPED POTATOES	132
BROCCOLI AND TOMATO CASSEROLE	133
CANDIED SWEET POTATOES	134
CHEESY CROCKPOT CORN	135
BROCCOLI CASSEROLE	136
VEGETABLE BAKE	137

COOKIES, BARS & CANDIES 139

TIGER BUTTER CANDY	139
GRAHAM CRACKER BROWNIES	140
MICROWAVE FUDGE	141
COOKIES FROM A CAKE MIX	142
ALMOND BARK COOKIES	144
ENGLISH TOFFEE TREATS	145
TING-A-LINGS	146

WORLD'S EASIEST COOKIES	147
APRICOT SNOWBALLS	148
DREAM BARS	149
CRISPY HONEY DROPS	150
SWEETHEART CHOCOLATE TRUFFLES	151
EASY PEANUT BUTTER COOKIES	152
TURTLES	153
CASHEW CLUSTERS	154
EASY ALMOND MACAROONS	155
QUICK, QUICK MACAROONS	156
KOLACHES	157
PEANUT BUTTER CHEWS	158
PEANUT BUTTER FUDGE	159
BUTTERSCOTCH CORNFLAKE TREATS	160
ENGLISH TOFFEE	161
PEANUT CLUSTERS	162
CHOW MEIN NOODLES	163
APRICOT CASHEW CLUSTERS	164
ALMOND COOKIES	165

CAKES & DESSERTS 167

PINEAPPLE TARTS	167
CAKE CONES	168
PULITZER PUDDING CAKE	169
QUICK AND EASY APPLE BUNDT CAKE	170
FRUIT COCKTAIL DESSERT	171
PINEAPPLE TURNOVERS	172

4 Ingredient Cookbook

You don't need an extensive pantry to cook up a meal that's tasty and sure to please the entire family. With just four ingredients, you can create everything from appetizers, main dishes and side dishes to breads and desserts.

Whether you're a busy parent on the run, a college student with little cash or a novice in the kitchen, you'll find loads of recipes to tempt your family's taste buds and keep your budget in check. These simple recipes are done in a snap and even a beginning cook can follow the simple directions to create a tasty meal.

Even if you love creating intricate, involved recipes, there's time when everyone need some go-to meal ideas that can be prepared and on the table fast. You'll use 4 Ingredient Cookbook's recipes again and again when you're pressed for time or aren't able to get to the store.

Here's a sample menu that everyone will enjoy and one that gives you plenty of time for relaxing with your friends and family.

Start your guests out with a savory and instant appetizer like One-minute Salsa and chips. When it's time to sit down for dinner, your guests will enjoy Cheddar Cheese Puffs and Creamy Cucumber Salad.

For your main dish, serve Chicken Breasts with Mushrooms on a bed of rice and finish your meal with Quick and Easy Apple Bundt Cake and a scoop of vanilla ice cream.

Your entire meal is created with recipes using four ingredients, so you'll be able to enjoy time with your guests and not spend the whole evening in the kitchen. Cleanup is a snap, as you won't be using every bowl and measuring cup in your kitchen to prepare your meal.

So, sit back and enjoy browsing through the 4 Ingredient Cookbook. You're sure to find plenty of great recipes to please your family and you'll save time and money by cooking the fast and easy, four ingredient way!

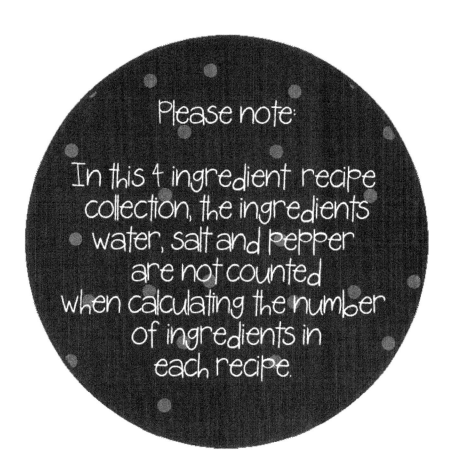

Please note:

In this 4 ingredient recipe collection, the ingredients water, salt and pepper are not counted when calculating the number of ingredients in each recipe.

menu

Snacks and Appetizers

Breadstick Pretzels
Crunchy Peanut Butter
Microwave Butter Crunch
One-minute Salsa
Pita Chips
Spicy Crockpot Peanuts
Fruit Dip
Pina Colada Fruit Dip
Baked Artichoke Dip

Onion Dip
Taco Dip
Oklahoma Chili Dip
Chinese Chicken Wings
Easy Cheese Ball
Butter Mushrooms
Tipsy Chicken Wings
Buffalo Chicken Dip
Crisp Tortilla Chips
Sweet N' Sour Wings

Snacks and Appetizers

Breadstick Pretzels

1 (11 oz.) refrigerated breadstick dough

1 egg, beaten

Pretzel salt or coarse sea salt

Preheat oven to 425 degrees F.

Form pretzel shapes with breadstick dough. Place on a greased cookie sheet. Brush each pretzel with egg and sprinkle with salt. Bake in the oven for 10 minutes at 425 degrees F until golden brown.

Crunchy Peanut Butter

2 1/2 cups salted peanuts

2 tablespoons margarine or butter, softened

Reserve 1/2 cup of the peanuts. Place remaining peanuts in blender. Cover and blend on low speed 10 seconds or until peanuts are chopped. Add margarine. Cover and blend on low speed 10 seconds; stop blender and scrape sides. Cover and blend on low speed 5 seconds; stop blender and scrape sides. Repeat 3 or 4 times or until peanut butter is almost smooth.

Cover and blend on high speed 1 minute. Add reserved peanuts. Cover and blend on medium speed 3 seconds. Place peanut butter in small bowl. Refrigerate about 30 minutes.

Yield: 1 cup peanut butter.

Microwave Butter Crunch

5 tablespoons butter or margarine

1/2 teaspoon salt

6 cups any type of Chex® cereal

1/3 cups grated parmesan cheese

Melt the butter or margarine in a large bowl in microwave for 50 to 60 seconds on High. Stir in salt. Add the cereal and stir to coat all pieces. Microwave on high 2 to 3 minutes until cereal is lightly toasted, stirring every half minute. Sprinkle cheese on top of the cereal mixture. Stir to coat all pieces. Spread on wax paper or parchment paper to cool.

Yield: 6 cups.

One-minute Salsa

1 (10 oz.) can diced tomatoes and green chiles, undrained

1 (14.5 oz.) can stewed tomatoes, undrained

1/2 teaspoon pepper

1/2 teaspoon garlic salt

Combine all ingredients in container of an electric blender; process 30 seconds. Serve salsa with tortilla chips.

Yield: 3 cups.

Pita Chips

4 (6-inch) whole wheat pita bread rounds

1/3 cup no-oil Italian dressing

1/2 cup grated Parmesan cheese

1 1/2 tablespoons sesame seeds

Preheat oven to 425 degrees F.

Separate each pita bread round into 2 pieces; cut each piece into 8 wedges. (Will make 64 wedges total). Brush inside of each triangle with Italian dressing. Place on ungreased baking sheets, dressing side up.

Combine Parmesan cheese and sesame seeds; sprinkle uniformly on triangles. Bake at 425 degrees F for 10 minutes or until lightly browned. Cool on wire racks. Store in an airtight container.

Yield: 64 chips.

Spicy Crockpot Peanuts

4 cups cocktail peanuts

1 (1 5/8 oz.) package chili seasoning mix

1/2 cup margarine, melted

Place the peanuts in a crockpot. Pour melted margarine over the nuts, then sprinkle with the chili mix. Stir until mixed well. Cover and cook on low for 2 to 2 1/2 hours.

Remove the crockpot lid and cook the nuts on high for 10 to 15 minutes. Pour out in single layer to cool on wax paper or parchment paper.

Fruit Dip

1 (8 oz.) package cream cheese

3/4 cup brown sugar, packed

1/4 cup sugar

1/4 teaspoon vanilla

Mix all ingredients together with a mixer. Use apples, oranges or berries with dip.

Pina Colada Fruit Dip

1 (8 oz.) can crushed pineapple (undrained)

3/4 cup skim milk

1 (3 oz.) package instant coconut cream pudding

1/2 cup fat-free sour cream

Combine all ingredients in a blender. Refrigerate for several hours. Serve with assorted fruits.

Onion Dip

1 (16 oz.) carton sour cream

1 (12 oz.) bag frozen chopped onions

1/2 cup mayonnaise

2 cups Parmesan cheese

Preheat oven to 350 degrees F.

Spray an 8x8" or 9x9" casserole dish with non-stick cooking spray. Mix all ingredients together and place in prepared casserole dish. Bake at 350 degrees F for 35 to 40 minutes. Serve with crackers.

Yield: 24 servings.

Taco Dip

1 lb. ground beef

2 lbs. Velveeta cheese

1 (16 oz.) jar picante sauce

Brown the ground beef and drain. Melt the Velveeta cheese in microwave and combine ground beef, cheese and picante sauce together. Keep warm in crockpot. Serve with tortilla chips.

Oklahoma Chili Dip

4 cups prepared chili with meat

8 oz. processed American or cheddar cheese, cubed

1 cup prepared green chilies with tomatoes (Ro-Tel)

1 to 2 tablespoons chili powder (optional)

Combine all the ingredients in a large saucepan and heat, stirring frequently, until the cheese is well mixed. Serve hot with tortilla chips.

Yield: 6 to 7 cups.

Chinese Chicken Wings

3 to 4 lb. chicken wings

1 (15 oz.) bottle soy sauce

1/2 cup sugar

Clean wings, snip tips, and discard. Mix soy sauce and sugar in a 9x13-inch baking dish. Add chicken wings, turn to coat, and marinate wings for 24 hours in refrigerator, turning often.

To cook - Pour off most of sauce. Cover dish tightly with foil. Bake at 250 degrees F for 2 hours. Remove foil during last 15 minutes of baking time to brown wings.

Easy Cheese Ball

1 (8 oz.) package cream cheese

1 (10 oz.) package sharp cheddar cheese spread

1 cup pecans, chopped

Let cream cheese and cheese spread package soften. When soft, mix together; form ball and roll in chopped pecans. Refrigerate.

Butter Mushrooms

1/2 cup butter or margarine

1 teaspoon garlic powder

1 envelope ranch dressing mix

1 package small button mushrooms, fresh

Melt butter or margarine in slow cooker. Add garlic powder, ranch dressing mix and mushrooms. Let simmer on medium for 1 hour.

Tipsy Chicken Wings

36 chicken wings or drumettes

1 cup soy sauce

1/2 cup vodka

1 tablespoon garlic salt

Preheat oven to 350 degrees F.

Combine soy sauce, vodka and garlic salt. Reserve 1/4 cup sauce for basting. Pour remainder of sauce over chicken pieces and marinate in refrigerator for 4 hours or overnight.

Bake chicken on a large cookie sheet at 350 degrees F for 40 minutes, turning occasionally and basting with soy sauce marinade.

Buffalo Chicken Dip

1 lb. chicken breast

1 (12 to 16 oz.) bottle ranch or blue cheese dressing

1 (8 to 16 oz.) bottle Frank's Red Hot Sauce

1 (8 to 12 oz.) package shredded cheddar cheese

Boil chicken breast until cooked all the way through and tender. Let cool in refrigerator. When cool enough to handle, shred chicken with fork. Combine shredded chicken, ranch or blue cheese dressing and hot sauce in a mixing bowl. (Use the amount of hot sauce to achieve your desired degree of spiciness.)

Pour mixture into 12x16" baking pan. Top with cheese and bake for 20 to 30 minutes at 350 degrees F. Serve with tortilla chips.

Crisp Tortilla Chips

4 (8-inch) flour tortillas

1 tablespoon margarine, melted

Preheat oven to 400 degrees F.

Brush tortillas lightly with margarine. Cut each tortilla into 12 pieces. Arrange in a single layer on ungreased cookie sheet. Bake at 400 degrees F for 8 to 10 minutes or until golden brown and crisp. (Chips will become crisper as they cool.)

Yield: 8 servings.

Sweet N' Sour Wings

3 packages chicken wings or drummies

1 (1.5 oz.) dry package onion soup mix

1 (8 oz.) bottle red Russian dressing

1 (12 oz.) jar apricot marmalade or jam

Preheat oven to 300 degrees F.

Mix ingredients: pour over chicken and bake 2 hours at 300 degrees F uncovered.

Bread and Rolls

Cheddar Cheese Puffs

1/2 cup all-purpose flour

1 cup shredded cheddar cheese

1/4 cup butter or margarine, softened

1/2 teaspoon ground mustard

Preheat oven to 400 degrees F.

In a bowl, combine cheese, butter or margarine and ground mustard; add flour and mix well. Roll into 1 inch balls. Place 1 inch apart on an ungreased baking sheet. Bake at 400 degrees F for 12 to 15 minutes or until lightly browned. Serve warm.

Yield: 2 dozen.

Little Olive Toasts

1 (1 lb.) loaf of French bread

1/3 cup green olives, chopped

1 (5 oz.) container garlic and herb spreadable cheese

1/3 cup ripe black olives, chopped

Slice French bread into 12 slices, each 1" thick. Place slices of bread on an ungreased baking sheet. Broil with tops 5 to 6 inches from heat until lightly toasted, about 30 to 60 seconds. Mix cheese and olives; spread on bread. Broil 1 to 2 minutes or until cheese is warm.

Yield: 12 slices.

Pepperoni Biscuits

2 cups Bisquick baking mix

2/3 cup milk

3/4 cup turkey pepperoni, chopped

Preheat oven to 450 degrees F.

Combine Bisquick and milk; mix with a fork until just moistened. Add pepperoni and mix just until combined. Place dough on lightly floured surface and knead 5 times.

Roll out to 1/2" thick and cut with a biscuit cutter. Spray a baking sheet with non-stick cooking spray, add biscuits and bake at 450 degrees F for 8 to 10 minutes, or until golden brown.

Yield: 10 biscuits.

Two Cheese Bread

1 (1 lb.) loaf French bread

1/2 cup margarine or butter, softened

1/4 cup crumbled blue cheese

1/4 cup shredded mozzarella cheese

Preheat oven to 350 degrees F.

Cut French bread in half horizontally. Mix together margarine or butter, blue cheese and mozzarella cheese. Spread cheese mixture on cut sides of bread. Reassemble loaf; cut into 1-inch slices. Wrap bread in heavy-duty aluminum foil. Bake at 350 degrees F for 20 minutes or until cheese is melted.

Yield: 12 slices.

Pesto Cheese Loaf

1 (1 lb.) loaf French bread

1/2 cup pesto sauce

1 cup shredded mozzarella cheese

1/2 cup tomato, chopped

Cut the loaf of bread horizontally in half. Place bread, cut sides up, on an ungreased baking sheet. Broil with tops 5 to 6 inches from heat until lightly toasted, about 1 minute. Spread pesto sauce on bread. Sprinkle with cheese and tomatoes. Broil 1 to 2 minutes more or until cheese is melted.

Yield: 12 slices.

Italian Muffins

2 tablespoons margarine or butter, softened

2 whole wheat English muffins, split

2 tablespoons grated Parmesan cheese

1/2 teaspoon Italian seasoning

Spread margarine or butter on muffin halves. Sprinkle each half with cheese and Italian seasoning. Place on rack in broiler pan. Broil with tops 4 inches from heat about 2 minutes or until light brown.

Yield: 4 servings.

Hawaiian Crescents

2 cans crescent rolls

4 to 6 slices ham

1 (8 oz.) can pineapple chunks, drained

Preheat oven to 400 degrees F.

Slice ham into 1/2 inch strips. Unroll one crescent at a time, placing a strip of ham and one pineapple chunk in the crescent. Roll up crescent according to package directions and place on cookie sheet. Bake at 400 degrees F for 10 to 12 minutes. Serve with Dijon mustard.

Yield: 16 servings.

Egg and Cheese Breakfast Burrito

6 eggs, lightly beaten

Salt and pepper to taste

5 (8-inch) flour or light wheat tortillas

3/4 cup shredded cheddar cheese

1/2 cup thinly sliced onions or green onions

Spray a large skillet with non-stick cooking spray. Add eggs, salt and pepper; cook and stir over medium heat until the eggs are completely set.

To assemble burritos, warm a few tortillas at a time in the microwave for 4 or 5 seconds. Spoon about 1/4 cup of egg mixture down the center of each tortilla; sprinkle with onions and cheese. Roll up burrito-style. Microwave each egg burrito for 20 seconds before serving. Serve with sour cream and salsa.

Yield: 5 burritos.

Optional: Add cooked bacon or sausage to egg mixture.

To Freeze: Wrap burritos individually in aluminum foil. Freeze for up to 1 month.

To use frozen burritos: Discard foil. Place burritos on a microwave-safe plate. Microwave at 50% power for 1 to 1-1/2 minutes or until heated through. Let stand for 20 seconds.

Main Dishes - Pork

Boneless Pork Chops

4 boneless pork chops

1 (15 oz.) can tomato sauce

1 teaspoon Worcestershire sauce

4 slices Velveeta cheese

Preheat oven to 350 degrees F.

Lightly spray the sides only of a 9x12 inch casserole dish with non-stick cooking spray. Pour the tomato sauce in the bottom, covering the bottom of the dish. Stir in the Worcestershire sauce. Add pork chops in a single layer on top of the tomato sauce.

Cover dish with aluminum foil and bake at 350 degrees F for 25 minutes. Remove from oven, turn each pork chop over and place one slice of Velveeta cheese on each chop. Bake, covered, for an additional 20 minutes or until pork chops are completely cooked.

Yield: 4 servings.

Ham Potato Casserole

1 cup shredded cheddar cheese

1/2 cup milk

2 cups cooked potatoes, diced

2 cups cooked ham, cubed

Preheat oven to 350 degrees F.

In a medium saucepan, heat cheese and milk. Stir constantly until cheese is melted. Remove from heat. Stir in potatoes and ham. Pour into an ungreased 1 1/2 quart casserole dish. Cover and bake at 350 degrees F for 45 minutes.

Yield: 4 servings.

Slow Cooker Barbecued Pork

3 to 4 lb. pork roast or Boston butt

Sugar

2 cups apple cider vinegar

1 (18 oz.) bottle of barbeque sauce

Trim excess fat from meat, roll meat in white sugar, put in slow cooker and add the vinegar. Cook on high for 1 hour. Reduce temperature to low and cook for 6 to 10 hours or on high for 4 to 5 hours. Remove from liquid. Shred with a fork. Add barbeque sauce.

Mustard Pork Chops

1 tablespoon spicy brown mustard

2 teaspoons lime juice

1/2 teaspoon ground cumin

12 to 16 oz. thin pork chops

Heat broiler. Line broiler pan with double thickness of aluminum foil. Whisk together mustard, lime juice and cumin. Wash and dry chops and trim away excess fat. Arrange on broiler pan and spread tops of chops with half of mustard mixture.

Broil chops 2 inches from source of heat for 5 to 6 minutes; turn and brush with remaining mustard mixture and broil for about 5 minutes more.

Yield: 2 servings.

Pork And Potato Bake

4 pork chops

4 medium potatoes

1 (10.5 oz.) can mushroom soup

1 (5 oz.) can evaporated milk

Preheat oven to 350 degrees F.

In a skillet, brown chops on both sides. Meanwhile slice or grate potatoes into thin slices like scalloped potatoes. Arrange potatoes in 8x8-inch baking dish. Top with browned chops. Add soup mixed with milk and bake at 350 degrees F for 1 hour or until done.

Slow Cooker Beer Chops

1 medium onion, chopped

2 pork chops, butterflied

1 (12 oz.) bottle or can of beer

2 chicken bouillon cubes

Sprinkle onions in the bottom of slow cooker. Place the chops on top of onions. Add beer and bouillon cubes. Cook on low for 6 to 8 hours.

Ham and Beans

1 lb. pinto beans

Ham (as much as desired)

Soak beans overnight; drain off water. Put beans and cubed ham in a slow cooker. Fill with enough water to cover the top of beans and ham. Cook on high 5 hours or 10 hours on low. Serve with corn bread.

menu

Main Dishes – Beef

Magic Meatballs
Easy Chili Casserole
Steak Bake
Goulash
Slow Cooker Burgundy Beef

Main Dishes -- Beef

Magic Meatballs

1 (32 oz.) package frozen meatballs

1 cup ketchup

1/3 cup jellied cranberry sauce or grape jelly

1/3 cup lemon juice

Place meatballs in a slow cooker. Mix ketchup, lemon juice and jelly; pour over meatballs. Heat on low for several hours.

Viennese Steak

1 1/2 lbs. round steak

1/4 cup water

1/2 teaspoon salt

1/4 teaspoon pepper

1/2 medium onion, chopped

1 (10.5 oz.) can cream of mushroom soup

Cut round steak into bite-size pieces. In a skillet, brown meat. Drain. Add water; sprinkle with salt and pepper and top with onions. Cook until hot. Put in crockpot. Cover crockpot and simmer until tender, at least 1 hour. Stir in soup and heat.

Easy Chili Casserole

1 lb. ground beef

1 (15 oz.) can chili

1 (16 oz.) bag tortilla chips, crushed

1 (6 oz.) package shredded cheese

Preheat oven to 400 degrees F.

Brown ground beef in skillet, stirring until crumbly; drain. Add chili. Cook until heated through, stirring occasionally. Layer tortilla chips and chili mixture in a casserole dish. Top with cheese. Bake at 400 degrees F until cheese is melted.

Yield: 4 to 6 servings.

Steak Bake

1 1/2 lbs. round steak

1 (1.5 oz.) package dry onion soup mix

1 (10.5 oz.) can condensed cream of mushroom soup

Preheat oven to 350 degrees F.

Cut round steak into serving pieces. Place in shallow baking dish. Sprinkle dry onion soup mix over steak. Spoon mushroom soup over top. Cover tightly with foil. Bake at 350 degrees F for 1 hour.

Yield: 5 servings.

Goulash

2 cups dry macaroni, boiled until done

1 lb. hamburger, browned

1 small onion, chopped

Salt and pepper to taste

1 (10.75 oz.) can tomato soup

Preheat oven to 350 degrees F.

Place cooked macaroni in a large casserole dish. Mix hamburger, onion, salt and pepper and soup. Pour over macaroni. Bake for 30 minutes in a 350 degree F oven.

Slow Cooker Burgundy Beef

4 to 5 lb. roast beef
1 cup Burgundy wine
1 (.7 oz.) package dry Italian dressing mix

Put the roast in slow cooker and sprinkle with dry seasoning. Pour wine over all. Cook beef in slow cooker on low for 8 hours or high for 4 hours, until done. Remove beef and shred. Return to juices and reheat. Serve on buns.

Main Dishes - Fish

Corn and Pineapple Salsa

1 cup frozen corn, thawed or fresh corn removed from cob

1/2 cup canned pineapple tidbits, drained (or fresh pineapple)

3/4 cup red onion, diced

1/2 fresh jalapeno or poblano chile

Salt and pepper to taste

Combine corn, pineapple, red onion and chile. Spray a foil-lined baking sheet with non-stick cooking spray. Add corn mixture to baking sheet in a single layer and broil for about 20 minutes, turning occasionally until the corn is slightly becoming charred. Season with salt and pepper. Serve with fish tacos or pile on top of servings of halibut.

Fish Tacos

4 hard taco shells

2 white fish fillets, cooked

3 tablespoons sour cream

2 tablespoons fresh cilantro, minced

Warm cooked fish in microwave. Divide the fish evenly into the 4 taco shells. Combine sour cream and cilantro. Divide evenly among the tacos.

Serve with corn and pineapple salsa (prior recipe) or tomato-based salsa. Add shredded lettuce, tomato and shredded Mexican cheese blend.

Baked Cod with Sour Cream

2 lbs. cod fillets

1/4 cup butter or margarine

1/2 cup grated Parmesan cheese

1 cup sour cream

Preheat oven to 400 degrees F.

Lay fish on greased, shallow baking pan. In small saucepan, melt butter. Stir in shredded cheese and sour cream. Spoon over fish. Bake at 400 degrees F for 20 minutes or until sauce topping is golden brown and fish is snowy white and easily flaked.

Yield: 4 servings.

Salmon Patties

1 can pink salmon, drained (reserve liquid)

3/4 cup cracker crumbs

Salt and pepper

2 eggs, beaten

Vegetable oil

Soak cracker crumbs in the liquid from the salmon to make them really soft. (If more liquid is required, add milk as needed.) Let stand 5 minutes. Add salt, pepper, eggs, and salmon. Mix thoroughly.

Using about 1/4 cup of mixture, shape into a patty and then heat enough vegetable oil in a heavy skillet to measure about half full. Add the patties to the moderately hot oil and fry until crispy brown, turning once.

Fish Fillets with Tomato Rice

1 lb. fresh fish fillets

1/2 cup rice, raw

1 teaspoon oregano

Freshly ground pepper

1/2 teaspoon salt

1 (1 lb.) can tomatoes

Preheat oven to 375 degrees F.

Place fresh fish fillets in a buttered baking dish. Pour rice around fish; sprinkle with oregano, pepper, and salt and pour tomatoes over fish and rice. If tomatoes are whole, break up with a fork. Cover dish with foil and bake in a 375 degrees F oven about 50 minutes, or until fish flakes easily and rice is tender.

Yield: 4 servings.

Broiled Fish with Dijon Sauce

1/2 cup mayonnaise

2 tablespoons Dijon mustard

3 tablespoons grated Parmesan cheese

1/8 teaspoon black pepper

1 lb. firm fish fillets

In a small bowl, combine mayonnaise, mustard, cheese, and pepper; mix well. Spread the mixture over the fillets. Broil the fish fillets for 5 to 7 minutes, depending on the thickness of the fish, or until fish flakes with a fork.

Yield: 3 to 4 servings.

Scallops Portuguese

1 lb. scallops

1/4 cup butter or margarine

1 garlic clove, minced

1/4 teaspoon salt

1/2 cup fresh parsley, chopped

1/8 teaspoon black pepper

Cut large scallops in half, pat dry with paper towels. Melt butter or margarine. Add garlic and salt, cook until garlic is golden brown. Add scallops and cook 5 to 7 minutes, stirring often. Sprinkle with pepper. Add parsley and cook 1 minute longer.

Yield: 4 servings.

Fried Scallops

1 lb. scallops

1 egg, beaten

1 cup crushed cracker crumbs or fine bread crumbs

Cover the scallops with boiling water and let them stand 3 minutes; drain and dry with paper towels, dip in egg then crumbs, and fry in hot oil until brown. (Or bake 15 minutes at 450 degrees F, turning to brown.)

Yield: 4 servings.

Broiled Fish Fillets and Fish Steaks

Fish fillets or fish steaks

Butter or French dressing

Salt and pepper to taste

Place fillets or steaks on a greased broiler pan. Brush fillets with butter or French dressing; season with salt and pepper. Place under broiler; broil 12 to 18 minutes, depending on the thickness of steaks or fillets. It is not necessary to turn during broiling.

Clam Mushroom Casserole

2 cups clams, chopped

2 cups mushrooms

1/2 cup margarine or butter, melted

1 teaspoon salt

1/2 teaspoon pepper

1 cup buttered bread crumbs

Preheat oven to 375 degrees F.

Spray a 2-quart casserole dish with non-stick cooking spray. Combine clams, mushrooms, margarine or butter, salt and pepper: add to casserole dish. Top with buttered bread crumbs. Bake at 375 degrees F for 15 to 20 minutes. Serve with buttered toast.

Fish-N-Chips Casserole

1 (5 oz.) can tuna, drained

1 (10.5 oz.) can cream of mushroom soup

2 (6 oz.) packages of potato chips, crushed

1 (14.5 oz.) can of English peas, drained (optional)

Preheat oven to 350 degrees F.

Combine tuna and soup. Spray a casserole dish with non-stick cooking spray and place a layer of potato chips in bottom; then a layer of tuna and soup (peas may be added). Now chips and then again tuna and soup. Top with thick layer of chips. Bake at 350 degrees F for 30 minutes.

Grilled Bourbon Honey Salmon

1 whole salmon fillet

1/2 cup bourbon

1 cup honey

1/2 teaspoon minced, fresh garlic

Salt and pepper to taste

On a medium heat grill, place salmon fillet skin side down on grill. Sprinkle salt and pepper over fillet. Cover the grill with lid or fish with aluminum wrap without touching fillet. Mix bourbon, honey and garlic. Brush honey mixture on fish. Coat well, cover.

Continue basting salmon every 2 minutes. While total cooking time varies with the thickness of the fish, it is relatively easy to determine its doneness. Simply lift the thickest part of the fish up from the grill with a tong or spatula, if it gives and slightly cracks on top it is done. Lift from grill and cut into serving portions.

Broiled Oysters

1 qt. select oysters

Buttered bread crumbs

Salt

Pepper

4 strips bacon, diced

1/4 cup butter or margarine

Pick over oysters and arrange in a shallow buttered baking pan. Sprinkle with salt and pepper. Sprinkle with bread crumbs and diced bacon; dot with butter or margarine. Broil 8 to 10 minutes or until oysters are brown and bacon is crisp. Serve garnished with lemon and parsley.

Tuna With Capers And Lemon Juice

2 teaspoons capers

1/2 lemon

12 oz. fresh tuna

Olive oil for brushing tuna

Cover a broiler pan with 2 sheets of aluminum foil. Drain and rinse capers. Dice lemon, leaving peel on, and combine with capers. Set aside.

Brush fish with olive oil. Measure fish at thickest point. Broil about 2 inches from source of heat, allowing 8 to 10 minutes per inch of thickness. When fish is cooked, sprinkle with capers and lemon and serve.

Yield: 2 servings.

Halibut Steaks Baked In Cream

2 lbs. halibut steaks

1 tablepoon lemon juice

1 onion, finely cut

1 teaspoon salt

1/2 teaspoon pepper

1 cup half and half

Preheat oven to 400 degrees F.

Place halibut steaks in single layer in a buttered baking dish. Mix remaining ingredients and pour over fish. Bake uncovered at 400 degrees F for 30 minutes or until fish flakes easily.

Yield: 6 servings.

menu

Main Dishes - Chicken

Chicken with Herb Butter
Cranberry Chicken
Chipotle Grilled Chicken
Chicken Breasts with Bacon
Microwave Baked Chicken
Chicken and Rice Casserole
Irish Chicken
Chicken Mozzarella
Lemon Chicken
Pepsi Chicken

Polo Asado
Mexicali Chicken
Vanilla Baked Chicken
Broiled Chicken
Crock Pot Chicken
Brilliant Chicken
Chicken Casserole
Asparagus Chicken
Deluxe
Easy Oven Dinner

Chicken Parmesan
Quick Chicken Goulash
Sunny Day Grilled Chicken
Salsa Chicken
Crockpot Stroganoff
Low-Calorie Juicy Chicken
Chicken Spaghetti
Chicken Bites
Broiled Chicken
Chicken Tacos

Skillet Chicken Breasts
Chicken Nuggets
Herb-Mustard Chicken
Chicken Breasts &
Mushrooms
Baked Chicken
Honey 'N Spice
Chicken
Chicken Cacciatore
Chicken Fajitas

Main Dishes - Chicken

Chicken with Herb Butter

4 bone-in chicken breasts

2 tablespoons margarine

Fines herbes

Preheat oven to 400 degrees F.

Clean and skin chicken. Lay chicken flat in casserole dish. Cover with fines herbes and butter. Bake at 400 degrees F for 45 minutes to 1 hour, basting occasionally.

Cranberry Chicken

8 chicken breasts, boneless and skinless

1 (15 oz.) can whole cranberry sauce

1 (8 oz.) small bottle fat free French dressing

1 (1.5 oz.) package Lipton dry onion soup mix

Preheat oven to 350 degrees F.

Arrange chicken breasts in 9x13" baking dish. Mix cranberry sauce and French dressing; add dry onion soup and pour mixture over chicken. Cover with foil and bake at 350 degrees F for 45 minutes. Remove foil and bake 10 to 20 additional minutes.

Yield: 8 servings.

Chipotle Grilled Chicken

4 chicken breasts, boneless

1/2 cup barbecue sauce

3 tablespoons onion, chopped

1 tablespoon chipotle chilies

In a small bowl, mix the barbecue sauce, onion and chilies together. Brush one side of each chicken breast with sauce. Grill chicken, sauce side down, for 5 to 8 minutes. Brush the other side of chicken breast with sauce, turn chicken and grill for an additional 5 to 8 minutes, or until chicken is tender.

Yield: 4 servings.

Chicken Breasts with Bacon

6 whole chicken breasts, boneless and skinless

Salt to taste

1 (8 oz.) package cream cheese, softened

10 to 12 green onions, chopped fine

12 slices bacon

Preheat oven to 350 degrees F.

Cut each chicken breast in half so there are 12 pieces of chicken. Lightly salt the chicken. Cut cream cheese into 12 chunky pieces. Press the onion into the cheese. Wrap chicken around each cheese chunk.

Lightly cook and drain the bacon. Wrap a slice of bacon around each breast, covering as much as possible. Secure with toothpicks. Bake uncovered at 350 degrees F for 1 hour or until tender.

Yield: 12 servings.

Microwave Baked Chicken

1 (3-lb.) chicken

Salt and pepper to taste

Lemon juice to taste

Rinse the chicken and pat dry inside and out. Sprinkle with salt, pepper and lemon juice. Place the chicken breast side down in a microwave-safe domed container. Microwave on High for 12 minutes. Turn the chicken breast side up. Microwave on High for 13 minutes. Let stand for 10 minutes before serving.

Yield: 2 to 4 servings.

Baked Chicken and Rice Casserole

4 to 6 bone-in chicken breasts

1 (6 oz.) box long grain and wild rice

2 cups hot water

1 (10.75 oz.) can cream of mushroom soup

In a greased 2 1/2 quart baking dish, mix 1 box rice and 2 cups hot water. Place chicken on top of rice. Bake, covered, at 375 degrees F for 1 1/2 hours. Dilute mushroom soup with water; mix well, then pour over chicken. Bake, uncovered, for 30 minutes, until chicken is browned.

Irish Chicken

6 to 8 chicken pieces, boneless and skinless, cut into serving pieces

1 egg, lightly beaten

1 cup dry potato flakes

1/2 cup margarine

Dip chicken piece in egg, then roll in potato flakes. Repeat with all chicken pieces. Melt 1/2 cup margarine in a shallow baking pan; place chicken in the pan and bake at 400 degrees F for 30 minutes. Turn chicken over and bake for 30 minutes longer.

Chicken Mozzarella

6 chicken breasts, boneless and skinless

1 (12 oz.) jar spaghetti sauce

6 slices mozzarella cheese

Spray a 9x13" baking dish with non-stick cooking spray. Place chicken breasts in baking dish. Cover with spaghetti sauce. Bake, covered, for 1 hour at 325 degrees F. Remove from oven.

Top each breast with 1 slice cheese. Return to oven and bake, uncovered, for 10 minutes longer. Serve with spaghetti or noodles if desired.

Lemon Chicken

4 chicken breasts, boneless and skinless

Juice of 1 or 2 lemons

Oregano or garlic powder to taste

Place chicken in a 9x13" greased baking dish. Squeeze lemon juice over each piece of chicken, then sprinkle your choice of oregano or garlic powder over each chicken breast. Bake at 325 degrees F for 45 minutes to 1 hour. Turn chicken once during cooking.

Pepsi Chicken

4 chicken breasts, skinless, with or without bones

1 cup barbecue sauce

1 (13 oz.) can Pepsi

2 tablespoons margarine or butter

Wash chicken. Turn electric skillet on 250 degrees F. Place 2 tablespoons margarine or butter in an electric skillet. Add chicken and brown. Combine and mix the barbecue sauce and Pepsi, then pour it over the chicken. Simmer at 250 degrees F for 1 hour. Turn chicken over and simmer for 1 hour longer if **bone-in** (just 15 to 20 minutes more if **boneless**) or until chicken is done.

STOVETOP INSTRUCTIONS – Put chicken in skillet with margarine or butter and brown. Combine and mix the barbecue sauce and Pepsi, then pour it over the chicken; stir. Cover and simmer 45 to 60 minutes or until chicken is done.

OVEN INSTRUCTIONS - Put chicken in skillet with margarine or butter and brown. Transfer chicken to a 9x13x2" baking dish. Combine and mix the barbecue sauce and Pepsi, then pour it over the chicken. Bake at 350 degrees F for one hour or until done.

Optional – onion strips can be added to the sauce mixture before cooking.

Chicken Parmesan

3 lbs. chicken pieces

1/2 cup Bisquick

1/2 cup grated parmesan cheese

Combine Bisquick and parmesan cheese. Coat chicken pieces in the mixture. Spray a casserole dish with non-stick cooking spray. Place chicken in casserole dish and bake, uncovered, for 30 minutes at 350 degrees F. Turn chicken over and bake for an additional 20 to 30 minutes, or until tender.

Quick Chicken Goulash

1 (10.5 oz.) can cream of mushroom soup

1 (14.5 oz.) can green beans, drained (save juice)

2 (12.5 oz.) cans chunk chicken breast

1 (3 oz.) can chow mein noodles

Stir together the soup, green beans and chicken. If the mixture needs thinning, add some of the green bean juice to thin. Cook until hot and serve over chow mein noodles.
Yield: 2 servings.

Sunny Day Grilled Chicken

6 to 8 bone-in chicken pieces

1/4 cup prepared mustard

1/4 cup honey

1/4 cup undiluted lemonade concentrate

Mix mustard, honey and lemonade concentrate. Place chicken on grill. Brush with 1/2 of the sauce. Grill for 15 minutes. Turn and brush with the rest of the sauce. Continue grilling for 20 to 30 minutes or until tender.

Yield: 4 to 6 servings.

Salsa Chicken

1 lb. chicken breasts, boneless and skinless

1 (1 oz.) package taco seasoning

1 (16 oz.) jar salsa

Water

Spray slow cooker with non-stick cooking spray. Sprinkle chicken with taco seasoning and place in slow cooker. Pour salsa over chicken. Add water if needed to create more broth. Cook in slow cooker on low for 8 to 10 hours or on high for 4 to 5 hours. Serve over rice or pasta.

Crockpot Stroganoff

2 to 4 skinless, boneless chicken breasts (cut into pieces)

1 (1.5 oz.) package dry onion soup mix

1 (10.5 oz.) can low-fat mushroom soup

1/2 cup no-fat sour cream

Mix onion soup and mushroom soup together. Stir in chicken pieces. Place in crockpot and cook on low for 6 hours. Just before serving stir in sour cream. Serve over rice or noodles.

Low-Calorie Juicy Chicken

1 1/2 lbs. chicken pieces, bone-in

1 cup V-8 juice (1 small can)

1/2 teaspoon oregano

1 teaspoon salt

1/4 teaspoon pepper

Wash and dry chicken pieces; place in shallow baking dish, skin side down. Mix together the V-8 juice, oregano, salt and pepper and pour over chicken; bake 1 hour at 350 degrees F. Turn chicken and bake an additional 1/2 hour or until liquid is absorbed by chicken.

Yield: 2 servings.

Chicken Spaghetti

1 (7 oz.) package thin spaghetti

1 (10 oz.) can diced tomatoes and green chilies, undrained

1 lb. processed American cheese, cubed

4 cups cooked chicken, cubed

Cook spaghetti according to package directions. Meanwhile, in a saucepan, combine the tomatoes and cheese; cook and stir until cheese is melted. Add chicken; heat through. Drain spaghetti; toss with cheese sauce.

Yield: 4 to 6 servings.

Chicken Bites

2 lbs. chicken breasts, boneless

3 cups dry bread stuffing mix, crushed

3 tablespoons orange juice

1 (16 oz.) bottle honey mustard salad dressing

Preheat oven to 400 degrees F.

Cut the chicken breasts into 1 inch pieces. Pour one cup of salad dressing in a bowl and dip the chicken in the dressing. Crush the stuffing into small pieces, put on a plate and roll the chicken in the stuffing. Use 2 cookie sheets for the chicken and bake at 400 degrees F for 15 minutes or until the chicken is no longer pink in the center.

Mix the orange juice and remaining salad dressing in a saucepan and cook over medium heat until heated through. Serve the hot dressing mixture with the chicken for dipping.

Yield: 8 servings.

Broiled Chicken

8 chicken pieces, bone-in

Juice of 2 lemons

Salt

3/4 cup butter, melted

Squeeze lemon over chicken and salt each piece liberally on each side. Preheat broiler and place chicken on the rack of the broiling pan, skin side down. Pour half the butter over chicken and broil 6 or 7 inches from the flame for 20 minutes. Turn, pour remaining butter over, and broil 20 minutes more. Pour pan juices over chicken before serving.

Yield: 8 servings.

Chicken Tacos

2 chicken breasts, boneless and skinless

10 corn tortillas

1/4 cup vegetable oil or canola oil

5 toothpicks, cut in half

Boil the chicken breasts with a little salt until cooked. Mince the chicken. Warm up tortillas. Place a spoonful of chicken on each tortilla, roll it up and hold the taco with 1/2 of a toothpick. In a large frying pan, heat the oil over medium-high heat and fry each taco until golden brown on each side (about 30 to 45 seconds on each side). Drain on paper towels.

Serve chicken tacos over bed of fine cut up lettuce with sour cream, salsa and guacamole on the side.

Yield: 5 servings.

Pollo Asado (Roast Chicken)

3 to 3 1/2 lb. whole roasting chicken

3 tablespoons Adobo

2 teaspoons paprika

6 tablespoons vegetable oil

Wash and dry the chicken. In a large bowl, mix Adobo, paprika and oil together. Put chicken in the bowl and coat it with the mixture. Cover bowl and place it in the refrigerator for at least two hours or overnight.

Preheat the oven to 350 degrees F. Remove the chicken from the marinade and place in a roasting pan, or on a rack for crispy skin. Roast the chicken for about 1 1/4 hours, basting it frequently with its own juices.

Yield: 4 servings.

Mexicali Chicken

2 chicken breasts, boneless and skinless

1 (11 oz.) can Mexicorn

1 (2.25 oz.) can sliced black olives

1 (8 oz.) can salsa, chunky style

Slice chicken into thin strips and sauté in a little oil until chicken turns white. Add corn, black olives and salsa; mix thoroughly until heated.

Serve with tortilla chips.

Yield: 2 servings.

Vanilla and Tarragon Baked Chicken

2 chicken breasts, bone-in with skins

3 to 6 fresh tarragon sprigs

Salt and pepper to taste

2 tablespoons chicken broth

1 tablespoon vanilla extract

Preheat oven to 350 degrees F.

Line a small baking pan with aluminum foil. Rinse chicken breasts; pat dry. Place in baking pan. Loosen skin gently with fingers. Place tarragon sprig under skin of each chicken breast. Sprinkle remaining tarragon over top. Season with salt and pepper.

Mix chicken broth and vanilla in a small bowl. Pour over chicken breasts. Seal baking pan securely in foil. Bake at 350 degrees F for 45 minutes, basting twice during baking. Drizzle basting liquid over chicken breasts; let stand for 5 to 10 minutes before serving.

Yield: 2 servings.

Broiled Chicken

6 to 8 chicken pieces, bone-in

1/4 cup vegetable oil

2 teaspoons salt

1 teaspoon paprika

1 1/2 teaspoons dry mustard

Preheat oven to 400 degrees F.

Thoroughly mix together oil, salt, paprika and dry mustard. Brush chicken with the sauce, once only. Put chicken skin side down in a shallow baking dish. Bake uncovered at 400 degrees F for 20 to 30 minutes. Turn skin side up and bake 40 minutes longer.

Yield: 4 servings.

Crock Pot Chicken

4 chicken breast halves, boneless and skinless

4 to 5 potatoes, peeled and cubed

1/4 onion, thinly sliced

Salt and pepper, to taste

1 (10.5 oz.) can cream of mushroom soup

Cut chicken into 1-inch pieces. Layer in crock pot potatoes, chicken, and then onion. Salt and pepper to taste. Layer cream of mushroom soup (undiluted) over top. Cook on slow setting 6 to 8 hours until done. Yield: 4 servings.

Brilliant Chicken

2 1/2 to 3 1/2-lbs. chicken pieces

1 egg, slightly beaten

1 cup dry potato flakes

1/2 cup butter or margarine

Preheat oven to 400 degrees F.

Melt butter or margarine in a shallow baking dish. Dip each chicken piece in egg and then roll in potato flakes. Place chicken in baking dish and bake for 30 minutes at 400 degrees F. Turn chicken over and bake for 30 minutes longer. Yield: 3 to 4 servings.

Chicken Casserole

6 to 8 chicken breasts, boneless

1/4 lb. Swiss cheese, sliced

1 (5 oz.) box stuffing mix

1 (10.5 oz.) can chicken broth

Preheat oven to 325 degrees F.

Arrange chicken in a 9x13" baking dish sprayed with non-stick cooking spray. Top with cheese slices. Sprinkle dry stuffing and seasoning packet from stuffing mix on cheese. Pour broth over all. Cover with foil and bake at 325 degrees F for 1 1/2 hours.

Asparagus Chicken Deluxe

4 cups precooked wild rice

2 cups creamed asparagus

2 cups cooked chicken, minced

Salt and pepper to taste

Mix all ingredients together and season with salt and pepper. Place in a saucepan and bring to a boil. Reduce heat and let simmer for 10 to 12 minutes.

Yield: 4 to 6 servings.

Easy Oven Dinner

1 cup wild rice, raw

6 to 8 chicken pieces, bone-in

1 (10.5 oz.) can cream of chicken soup

1 1/2 cans water

Preheat oven to 350 degrees F.

Place chicken in a large oven-proof casserole dish. In a bowl, mix soup with 1 1/2 cans water. Pour wild rice and diluted soup mixture over chicken. Cover and bake at 350 degrees F for about 2 hours or until chicken is tender and cooked through. Check during baking time, making sure there is enough liquid. Add more as needed.

Yield: 4 to 6 servings.

Skillet Chicken Breasts

4 chicken breast halves, bone-in

1/4 teaspoon seasoned salt

1/8 teaspoon black pepper

1/8 teaspoon paprika

1 1/3 cups water

Sprinkle the skin of each chicken breast with salt, pepper and paprika. In a large skillet, add water and bring to a boil. Add the chicken, skin side up. Cover and simmer on medium heat for 20 to 30 minutes or until chicken is tender and juices run clear.

Yield: 4 servings.

Chicken Nuggets

4 chicken breast halves, skinless and boneless

1 (5 oz.) can evaporated skim milk

8 oz. crushed potato chips

Preheat oven to 400 degrees F.

Cut chicken into 2 inch pieces. Spray a large baking sheet with non-stick cooking spray. Dip chicken in milk then roll in potato chips. Place on baking sheet and bake at 400 degrees F for 30 minutes until chicken is golden brown and no longer pink in the center.

Yield: 4 servings.

Grilled Herb-Mustard Chicken

3 to 3 1/2-lbs. chicken pieces, bone-in with skin

1/2 cup plain yogurt

2 tablespoons spicy brown mustard

1 teaspoon dried thyme

Place chicken pieces in a 9x13" baking dish, skin side up and thickest parts to outside edges. Cover with plastic wrap, turning one corner back to vent. Microwave on high 8 to 10 minutes or until outside edges of chicken begin to cook.

Combine yogurt, mustard and thyme. Grill chicken covered, skin sides down, 4 to 6 inches from medium heat for 10 minutes. Turn chicken and brush with yogurt mixture. Cover and grill 10 to 15 minutes longer, brushing frequently with yogurt mixture, until done.

Yield: 6 servings.

Chicken Breasts with Mushrooms

2 chicken breasts, bone-in with skin

1/2 (10.5 oz.) can cream of mushroom soup

1 (4 oz.) can mushroom pieces (or fresh pieces)

Mix all ingredients in a slow cooker and cook for 3 1/2 to 4 1/2 hours on low or for 7 to 9 hours on high. Remove skin on chicken breasts before serving or during last few hours of cooking.

Serve over rice.

Baked Chicken

6 chicken breasts, boneless

1 teaspoon salt

1 (12 oz.) can apricot nectar

1 (1.5 oz.) envelope dry onion soup mix

Preheat oven to 325 degrees F.

Arrange chicken in a shallow baking pan. Sprinkle with salt. Pour apricot nectar over chicken and sprinkle with 1/2 to 3/4 envelope of soup mix. Cover tightly with foil. Bake at 325 degrees F for 2 hours. Lift foil and let brown for a few minutes.

Honey 'N Spice Chicken

2 to 2 1/2 lbs. chicken pieces

1/2 cup Heinz 57 sauce

2 tablespoons honey

1/4 cup butter or margarine, melted

Preheat oven to 375 degrees F.

Brush chicken pieces with melted butter or margarine; place in shallow baking dish. Bake at 375 degrees F for 40 minutes. Combine Heinz 57 and honey. Turn chicken over and brush with half of sauce. Bake 15 to 20 minutes longer or until tender. Brush again.

Yield: 4 to 5 servings.

Chicken Cacciatore

3 to 4 chicken breasts, skinless and boneless

1 (15 oz.) jar chunky spaghetti sauce

1 green pepper, cut in strips

1 tablespoon vegetable oil

Heat oil in skillet. Cut chicken into cubes. Add chicken to skillet, turning frequently to brown all sides until center is no longer pink, about 10 minutes. Drain. Add spaghetti sauce and green peppers to chicken. Bring to a boil, cover skillet and cook on low for 10 minutes, or until heated through. To serve, place chicken on a platter and pour sauce over it.

Yield: 3 to 4 servings.

Chicken Fajitas

1 1/2 lbs. chicken breasts, boneless and skinless

1 cup picante sauce

1/4 cup vegetable oil

1 teaspoon lemon juice

1/8 teaspoon of pepper

Slice chicken into thin strips. Combine picante sauce, oil, lemon juice and pepper. Place in large resealable plastic bag. Add chicken. Marinate in refrigerator at least 3 hours, up to 24 hours, turning several times.

Drain chicken and grill until thoroughly cooked. Serve with flour tortillas, chopped tomatoes, onions, shredded cheese, sour cream or ranch dressing.

Salads

Buttermilk Salad

1 (6 oz.) box strawberry jello

1 (20 oz.) can crushed pineapple (not drained)

2 cups buttermilk

1 (9 oz.) carton refrigerated whipped topping

Mix jello and pineapple with juice in a large saucepan, bring to a boil. Remove from heat. When mixture is cold, stir in buttermilk and add whipped topping. Pour into a 13x9" dish. Refrigerate and serve cold.

Snickers Salad

5 (1.86 oz.) Snickers® candy bars cut into little pieces

8 granny smith apples, peeled and diced

1 (16 oz.) carton refrigerated whipped topping

1 (5.9 oz.) box instant vanilla pudding (dry)

Mix all ingredients together. Refrigerate and serve cold.

Tomato and Corn Salad

1 (15.25 oz.) can whole kernel corn, drained

1 medium tomato, diced

2 tablespoons onion, chopped

1/3 cup mayonnaise

(optional - 1/4 teaspoon dill weed)

In a medium bowl, combine all ingredients; mix well. Cover and refrigerate until serving.

Yield: 4 servings.

Creamy Cucumbers

2 medium cucumbers

1/2 cup sour cream

1 tablespoon vinegar

1 tablespoon onion, finely chopped

Salt and pepper to taste

Peel cucumbers and cut into 1/4" thick slices. In a medium bowl, combine sour cream, vinegar and onion. Season with salt and pepper to taste. Stir in cucumbers.

Yield: 4 servings.

Pistachio Salad

1 (9 oz.) carton refrigerated whipped topping

1 (3.4 oz.) box instant pistachio pudding

2 cups miniature white marshmallows

1 (20 oz.) can crushed pineapple (not drained)

In a large bowl, mix whipped topping and pudding. Add marshmallows and pineapple including juice. Chill at least 2 hours.

Pink Fluff

1 (3 oz.) package cream cheese, softened

1 (21 oz.) can cherry pie filling

1 (16 oz.) carton refrigerated whipped topping

1 (20 oz.) can pineapple tidbits, with juice

Mix all 4 ingredients in large mixing bowl with an electric mixer. Refrigerate for 2 to 3 hours before serving.

Tuna Salad

1 (9 oz.) package refrigerated tortellini

1 (12 oz.) can tuna, drained

1 (16 oz.) package frozen broccoli, cauliflower and carrots, thawed and drained

1/2 cup creamy Parmesan dressing

Cook pasta according to package directions. Drain pasta; rinse with cold water. In a large bowl, mix pasta, tuna and vegetables. Add dressing and toss until mixed. Refrigerate, covered, for 2 hours.

Yield: 6 servings.

Red Cinnamon Apple Salad

2/3 cup red hot cinnamon candies

1 cup hot water

1 (3 oz.) package lemon jello

1 1/2 cup applesauce

Pour hot water over red hot candies and stir until dissolved. Add lemon jello and stir until dissolved. Add applesauce and pour entire mixture into a casserole dish or jello mold. Chill in refrigerator until firm.

Yield: 6 servings.

menu
Side Dishes

Jalapeno Crockpot Corn
Baked Fries
Broccoli & Chicken Potatoes
Broccoli & Tomato Casserole

Twice-Baked Potatoes
Green Beans And Salsa
Zesty Red Potatoes
Simple Macaroni And Cheese
Poppy-Seed Bowtie Pasta
Glazed Baby Carrots

Candied Sweet Potatoes
Cheesy Crockpot Corn
Broccoli Casserole
Vegetable Bake

Au Gratin Potatoes
Cran-Apple Sauce
Water Chestnuts and Peas
Corn on the Cob
Fried Macaroni

Side Dishes

Twice-Baked Potatoes

4 to 6 baking potatoes

1/2 cup sour cream or plain yogurt

1/2 cup shredded Cheddar cheese

Preheat oven to 425 degrees F.

Scrub potatoes, rub with olive oil and place in a baking pan. Bake for 1 hour at 425 degrees F or until tender. Cut a slit in the potatoes and scoop out the centers. Mash potatoes; mix with sour cream or yogurt and shredded cheese, then stuff the potatoes with mixture. Bake at 350 degrees F for 15 to 20 minutes.

Green Beans And Salsa

1 (14.5-oz.) can cut green beans

1/2 to 3/4 cup thick and chunky salsa

(optional - 1 tablespoon fresh cilantro, chopped)

Heat green beans in medium saucepan until hot; drain well. Stir in salsa; cook 1 to 2 minutes or until thoroughly heated. Sprinkle with cilantro.

Yield: 6 servings.

Zesty Red Potatoes

6 medium red potatoes, halved and sliced thin

1 small onion, halved and sliced thin

1/2 cup butter or margarine, melted

1/2 teaspoon crushed red pepper flakes

1/8 teaspoon salt

Preheat oven to 400 degrees F.

Arrange potatoes and onion in a 9x9" baking dish. Combine butter or margarine, pepper flakes and salt; sprinkle over potatoes and onion. Cover and bake at 400 degrees F for 25 minutes. Uncover; bake 15 to 20 minutes longer or until potatoes are tender.

Yield: 6 to 8 servings.

Simple Macaroni and Cheese

3 tablespoons margarine or butter

2 1/2 cups uncooked macaroni

1/2 teaspoon salt

1/8 teaspoon pepper

1/2 lb. sharp cheddar cheese, shredded

4 cups milk

Preheat oven to 350 degrees F.

Melt margarine or butter in a large baking dish. Pour uncooked macaroni into melted butter. Stir until macaroni is well covered. Add salt, pepper, cheese and milk; stir until mixed well. Bake at 350 degrees F for 45 to 60 minutes. Do not stir while baking.

Poppy-Seed Bowtie Pasta

8 oz. bowtie pasta

3 tablespoons butter or margarine

1 teaspoon poppy seeds

1/2 teaspoon salt

1/4 teaspoon pepper

Cook noodles according to package directions; drain. Toss gently with butter or margarine, poppy seeds and salt and pepper.

Yield: 4 servings.

Glazed Baby Carrots

1 lb. fresh or frozen whole baby carrots

2 tablespoons butter or margarine

1/4 cup brown sugar, packed

Place carrots in a saucepan with water just to cover carrots; bring to a boil. Cover and cook for 10 minutes until tender but still crisp. Drain; remove from heat and keep warm. In the same pan, heat butter and sugar until bubbly. Return carrots to pan. Toss to coat; heat through.

Yield: 4 servings.

Au Gratin Potatoes

4 large russet potatoes, peeled

1 (10.75) can of condensed cheddar cheese soup

2 tablespoons margarine or butter

1/2 cup American cheese

Preheat oven to 350 degrees F.

Boil about 4 cups of potatoes until tender. Drain and slice into a casserole dish.

Mix soup, butter or margarine and cheese together. Pour over potatoes. (Thin with a little milk if seems too thick.) Bake at 350 degrees about 15 minutes until cheese melts and becomes bubbly.

Cran-Apple Sauce

1 (8 oz.) can jellied cranberry sauce

1 (24 oz.) jar applesauce

Whipped topping

In a bowl, break up the cranberry sauce with a fork. Add applesauce and mix well. Refrigerate until serving. Garnish with whipped topping.

Yield: 4 to 6 servings.

Water Chestnuts and Peas

1 (10 oz.) package frozen peas or 2 cups fresh peas

1 (8 oz.) can sliced water chestnuts, drained

1 (14.5 oz.) can chicken broth

1 tablespoon butter or margarine

(optional - 1/8 teaspoon salt and sugar)

In a medium saucepan, cook water chestnuts and peas in chicken broth for 5 minutes or until peas are tender. Drain; add butter and seasonings if desired.

Yield: 4 servings.

Microwave Corn on the Cob

4 ears husked sweet corn

1/4 cup butter or margarine, softened

1 teaspoon snipped chives

Wrap each ear of corn separately in waxed paper. Microwave on High for 12 to 14 minutes, rotating halfway through cooking time. In a small bowl, combine butter or margarine and chives until blended. Serve with corn.

Yield: 4 servings.

Fried Macaroni

2 cups elbow macaroni

2 quarts water

2 or 3 tablespoons butter or margarine

Salt and pepper to taste

Cook macaroni in 2 quarts water. Drain. Melt butter or margarine over medium heat in heavy skillet. Add cooked, drained macaroni. Fry as you would potatoes, turning as the macaroni browns. Salt and pepper to taste.

Jalapeno Crockpot Corn

1 (20 oz.) package frozen corn

1 (8 oz.) jar processed cheese sauce, jalapeno

1 (8 oz.) carton sour cream

1 (4 oz.) can chopped green chilies

Combine corn, processed cheese sauce, sour cream and chopped green chilies in crockpot. Cook on low setting 3 to 4 hours, stirring occasionally.

Baked Fries

5 medium baking potatoes

1/4 cup vegetable oil

Salt and pepper to taste

Preheat oven to 450 degrees F.

Slice potatoes into about 1/8" thick; place in ice water. Drain; pat dry with paper towels. Pour oil in a 9x13" baking dish. Arrange potatoes in a single layer, turning to coat. Season with salt and pepper. Bake at 450 degrees F for 15 minutes or until potatoes are tender.

Yield: 4 servings.

Cheesy Broccoli and Chicken-Topped Potatoes

2 medium baking potatoes

1 (10 oz.) package frozen cut broccoli in cheese flavored sauce

2/3 cup cubed cooked chicken breast

Prick potatoes with a fork. Microwave potatoes on HIGH for 5 to 8 minutes or until tender. Set aside. Microwave broccoli following package directions. Warm chicken if cold and place in a medium bowl. Add broccoli and cheese sauce; mix well. Cut the top of each potato open and spoon broccoli/chicken mixture on potatoes.

Yield: 2 servings.

Broccoli and Tomato Casserole

3 (10 oz. each) packages frozen broccoli, thawed and drained

3 large tomatoes, peeled and sliced

2/3 cup grated Parmesan cheese

2 cups mayonnaise

Preheat oven to 325 degrees F.

Spray a 10 inch round casserole dish with non-stick cooking spray. Arrange broccoli in the bottom of the dish; top with tomato slices. Combine Parmesan cheese and mayonnaise together. Spread cheese mixture over tomato slices. Bake at 325 degrees F for 50 to 60 minutes, or until nicely browned.

Yield: 8 to 10 servings.

Candied Sweet Potatoes

4 sweet potatoes

1/2 cup granulated sugar

1/2 cup butter or margarine

1 teaspoon vanilla extract

Peel potatoes and rinse. Cut potatoes into fourths. Melt butter or margarine in a skillet. Place potatoes in melted butter. Add granulated sugar and vanilla. Cover and simmer on low heat for 30 minutes.

Cheesy Crockpot Corn

1/2 cup margarine or butter

1 (8 oz.) package cream cheese

1/4 cup sugar

2 (1 lb. each) packages frozen kernel corn

Spray a crockpot with non-stick cooking spray. Place margarine or butter and cream cheese in bottom of crockpot. Add corn, then sugar. Cook on high for 2 hours or on low for 4 hours, stirring occasionally.

Broccoli Casserole

1 1/2 cups cooked rice

1 (10.5 oz.) can cream of mushroom soup

1 (10 oz.) package frozen broccoli, chopped and cooked

1 (15 oz.) jar processed cheese sauce

Preheat oven to 350 degrees F.

Mix together rice, mushroom soup, broccoli and cheese sauce. Pour into a large casserole dish and bake at 350 degrees F for 20 minutes.

Vegetable Bake

15 to 20 small new potatoes, scrubbed with skins on

8 to 10 carrots, sliced

2 large onions, sliced

1/4 cup butter or margarine

Preheat oven to 325 degrees F.

Fill baking dish with new potatoes. Layer sliced carrots over top, then onions. Dot with butter or margarine. Bake at 325 degrees F, covered, for 2 hours or until potatoes are tender.

menu
Cookies, Bars & Candies

Tiger Butter Candy
Graham Cracker Brownies
Microwave Fudge
Cookies from a Cake Mix
Almond Bark Cookies
English Toffee Treats

Cashew Clusters
Easy Almond Macaroons
Quick Macaroons
Kolaches
Peanut Butter Chews

Ting-A-Lings
World's Easiest Cookies
Apricot Snowballs
Dream Bars
Crispy Honey Drops
Chocolate Truffles
Peanut Butter Cookies
Turtles

Peanut Butter Fudge
Butterscotch Cornflake Treats
English Toffee
Peanut Clusters
Chow Mein Noodles
Apricot Cashew Clusters
Almond Cookies

Cookies, Bars & Candies

Tiger Butter Candy

1 (24 oz.) package almond bark

1/2 cup crunchy peanut butter

1 1/2 cups semi-sweet chocolate chips

Line a cookie sheet with aluminum foil. In a saucepan, melt almond bark and peanut butter together over low heat. While that is melting, melt the chocolate chips in a microwave at 50% power, stirring every 30 seconds.

When melted, pour the almond bark mixture on the foil lined cookie sheet. Drizzle the melted chocolate chips over the almond bark mixture and make swirly designs with a spoon. Refrigerate until cold; break into pieces.

Graham Cracker Brownies

6 oz. semi-sweet chocolate chips

2 cups graham cracker crumbs

1 (14 oz.) can sweetened condensed milk

1 teaspoon baking powder

Preheat oven to 350 degrees F.

In a large bowl, combine chocolate chips, graham cracker crumbs, condensed milk and baking powder. Spray an 8x8" baking dish with non-stick cooking spray. Spread mixture evenly in baking dish. Bake at 350 degrees F for 30 minutes or until toothpick inserted in center comes out clean.

Microwave Fudge

18 oz. package semi-sweet chocolate chips

1 (14 oz.) can sweetened condensed milk

1 teaspoon vanilla

1 1/2 cups pecans

Mix chocolate chips and condensed milk together; microwave for one minute on High. Stir, microwave 1 1/2 minutes more. Add vanilla and pecans. Pour in an 8x8" buttered dish and refrigerate.

Cookies from a Cake Mix

1 (17 oz.) package any flavor cake mix

1/2 cup oil

2 eggs

Preheat oven to 325 degrees F.

In a large bowl, mix dry cake mix, oil and eggs. Spray a cookie sheet with non-stick cooking spray. Drop batter by teaspoonfuls onto cookie sheet. Bake at 325 degrees F for 10 minutes. Cool on cookie sheet for 1 minute. Remove to wire rack to cool completely.

Variations:

Double Chocolate – Use a chocolate cake mix and add 1 to 2 cups chocolate chips. Combine and bake as directed above.

Chocolate Chip – Use a yellow cake mix and add 2 cups chocolate chips. Combine and bake as directed above.

Coconut Almond – Use a white cake mix and add 1 cup shredded coconut and 1 teaspoon almond extract. Combine and bake as directed above.

Banana Spice – Use a spice cake mix and add 1/2 cup mashed banana and 1/2 cup chopped pecans. Combine and bake as directed above.

Lemon Oatmeal – Use a lemon cake mix, only 1 egg and add 1/4 cup packed brown sugar and 3/4 cup oats. Combine and bake as directed above.

Yield: 4 to 5 dozen.

Almond Bark Cookies

1/2 large package almond bark

2 cups broken stick pretzels

2 cups crispy rice cereal

1 or 2 cups dry roasted peanuts

Melt almond bark in microwave. Add the pretzels, cereal and peanuts; mix well. Drop by tablespoons on wax paper to cool.

English Toffee Treats

1 cup butter

1 1/2 cups brown sugar, packed

2 cups whole walnuts

1 (12 oz.) package semi-sweet chocolate chips

Mix the butter and brown sugar in a saucepan. Boil for 7 minutes. Lay out the walnuts on a greased baking sheet. Pour the butter mixture over the nuts. Sprinkle the chocolate chips on top. Let set until soft and spread chocolate over candy. Cool, break into pieces.

Ting-A-Lings

1 (12 oz.) package semi-sweet chocolate chips

4 cups corn flakes

Melt chocolate chips; cool to room temperature. Gently stir in corn flakes until well coated. Drop by spoonfuls onto waxed paper or foil. Refrigerate until set, about 2 hours.

World's Easiest Cookies

1 cup peanut butter

1 cup sugar

1 egg

Preheat oven to 350 degrees F.

Mix all 3 ingredients together. Drop by spoonfuls or shape into small balls on cookie sheet. Bake at 350 degrees F for 10 to 12 minutes.

Apricot Snowballs

1 1/2 cups dried apricots

2 cups coconut (ground)

2/3 cups sweetened condensed milk

Powdered sugar

Combine dried apricots, coconut and milk. Roll into small balls; then roll in confectioners' sugar. Refrigerate.

Dream Bars

1 package (22 singles) graham crackers, crushed

1 cup chocolate chips

1 cup coconut

1 can sweetened condensed milk

Preheat oven to 350 degrees F.

Mix graham cracker crumbs, chocolate chips and coconut together. Add condensed milk; mix well. Spray an 8x8" baking dish with non-stick cooking spray. Place mixture in baking dish and bake at 350 degrees F for 20 minutes or until golden brown.

Crispy Honey Drops

1/2 cup honey

1/4 cup margarine or butter

3 cups cornflake cereal

1/2 cup peanuts

Line a baking sheet with waxed paper. In a large saucepan, combine honey and margarine or butter. Bring to a boil; boil for 2 minutes. Remove from heat. Add cornflakes and peanuts; stir until well coated. Drop by rounded tablespoonfuls onto baking sheet. Refrigerate until set. Store in refrigerator.

Yield: 24 cookies.

Sweetheart Chocolate Truffles

1 1/2 lb. milk chocolate

1/3 cup heavy cream

1/3 cup half and half

1 1/2 teaspoons vanilla extract

Melt milk chocolate in double boiler over hot water; beat until smooth. Bring cream and half and half just to the simmering point in saucepan. Cool to 130 degrees F. Add to melted chocolate; beat until smooth. Stir in vanilla. Cool. Beat until light and fluffy. Chill until firm. Shape into small balls. If desired, dip into melted dipping chocolate or roll in cocoa.

Easy Peanut Butter Cookies

1 large egg, beaten

1 cup crunchy peanut butter

1 cup sugar

36 milk chocolate kisses, unwrapped

Preheat oven to 350 degrees F.

Combine egg, peanut butter and sugar; shape into 3/4-inch balls. Place on ungreased cookie sheets; bake at 350 degrees F for 10 minutes. Remove from oven and quickly press a chocolate kiss in the center of each cookie; remove to wire racks to cool.

Yield: 3 dozen.

Turtles

1 lb. cashew nuts

1 (1-lb.) package caramels

8 oz. semisweet chocolate, melted

Spray a cookie sheet with non-stick cooking spray. On cookie sheet, arrange groups of 4 cashew nuts, total of 60 groups. Melt caramels in top of double boiler with 2 tablespoons water. Let caramel syrup cool 2 to 3 minutes in pan. Spoon a tablespoon of liquid caramel over cashew nut group. Let cool for 10 minutes. Spoon melted chocolate over top of the caramel. Allow to cool completely.

Yield: 60 turtles.

Cashew Clusters

9 oz. semi-sweet chocolate

1/2 cup cashews

1/2 cup Craisins® sweetened dried cranberries

In a double boiler, melt chocolate. Remove from heat and let cool for 5 minutes. Stir in cashews and cranberries. Drop by teaspoonfuls onto a buttered cookie sheet. Let harden at room temperature or chill in refrigerator.

Yield: About 16 clusters.

Easy Almond Macaroons

8 oz. almond paste

1 cup granulated sugar

2 egg whites

1 teaspoon almond extract

Preheat oven to 325 degrees F.

Cut almond paste into small pieces and gradually beat in sugar. Add egg whites and almond extract; beat well. Drop by rounded teaspoonfuls on a non-stick baking sheet, or on a cookie sheet lined with parchment paper, placing drops about two inches apart. Bake at 325 degrees F for 20 to 30 minutes, or until cookies are lightly browned.

Yield: 50 cookies.

Quick, Quick Macaroons

1 (16 oz.) package grated coconut

1 (14 oz.) can sweetened condensed milk

2 teaspoons almond or vanilla extract

Preheat oven to 350 degrees F.

Mix coconut and condensed milk; stir in almond or vanilla extract. Drop by teaspoonfuls on a greased or parchment paper lined cookie sheet. Bake at 350 degrees F for 10 to 12 minutes.

Yield: 4 dozen cookies.

Kolaches

1 cup margarine

1 (8 oz.) package cream cheese

2 cups flour

1 (21 oz.) can pie filling (apricot, prune, etc.)

Preheat oven to 350 degrees F.

With margarine and cream cheese at room temperature, cream together. Add flour gradually. Chill. Using about 1/3 dough at a time roll out very thin on floured board. Cut with desired sized cutter (I use a juice glass). Make imprint with finger in center and add pie filling.

Place on ungreased cookie sheet. Bake at 350 degrees F for 15 minutes or until lightly browned. When cooled sprinkle with confectioners' sugar, if desired.

Peanut Butter Chews

1 cup peanut butter

1 cup corn syrup

1 1/4 cups confectioners' sugar

2 cups instant nonfat dry milk

Mix all ingredients in a bowl. Press into a pie or a cake pan. Let set. Cut into 24 pieces. Keep refrigerated.

Peanut Butter Fudge

1 cup creamy peanut butter

1 (6-oz.) package semisweet chocolate chips

1/2 cup margarine or butter

1 cup sifted confectioners' sugar

In a saucepan over low heat, cook peanut butter, chocolate chips and margarine or butter, stirring constantly until melted. Remove from heat. Add confectioners' sugar, and mix until smooth. Pour into a buttered 8x8" pan; chill until firm. Keep refrigerated.

Butterscotch Cornflake Treats

6 cups cornflakes

1 (12 oz.) package butterscotch morsels

1 cup creamy peanut butter

Melt butterscotch morsels and peanut butter over low heat. Add cornflakes and mix until cereal is coated. Drop by tablespoon onto waxed paper. Let stand and harden about one hour. Store in airtight container.

Yield: 40 treats.

English Toffee

1 cup butter

1 cup sugar

3 tablespoons water

1 tablespoon vanilla

3 (1.55 oz. each) chocolate candy bars

Put all ingredients in a heavy saucepan. Cook on medium high until brown, about 10 or 11 minutes. Stir constantly while mixture is boiling. Pour onto a greased cookie sheet. While mixture is still hot, put candy bars broken into pieces on top. Spread over toffee mixture. Sprinkle with nuts, if desired.

Peanut Clusters

1 (12 oz.) package semi-sweet chocolate chips

1 (14 oz.) package vanilla almond bark

12 oz. Spanish peanuts

Combine chocolate chips and almond bark in a microwave-safe bowl. Melt in microwave, about 3 to 4 minutes, stirring often. Remove from microwave and stir in peanuts. Drop by teaspoonfuls on waxed paper. Let stand 30 minutes.

Chow Mein Noodles

1 (6 oz.) package butterscotch or chocolate chips

1/2 cup peanut butter, chunky

1 (3 oz.) can chow mein noodles

1 cup miniature marshmallows

Melt chips and peanut butter in saucepan over low heat, stirring constantly. Remove from heat and add chow mein noodles and miniature marshmallows. Drop by teaspoonful on waxed paper. Chill.

Apricot Cashew Clusters

1 (11.5 oz.) package milk chocolate chips

1 cup salted cashews, chopped

1 cup dried apricots, chopped

In a microwave-safe bowl, melt the chocolate chips, stirring often until melted; stir until smooth. Stir in cashews and apricots. Drop by rounded tablespoonfuls onto waxed paper-lined baking sheets. Chill until set, about 15 minutes.

Yield: 2 1/2 dozen.

Almond Cookies

1 1/3 cups blanched (skinless) almonds

2/3 cup granulated sugar

1/8 teaspoon salt

2 egg whites

Preheat oven to 400 degrees F.

Blend blanched almonds in blender until a fine consistency. Mix with sugar and salt. With an electric mixer, beat egg whites until they form stiff peaks. Fold into almond mixture. Drop by heaping teaspoonfuls onto a greased cookie sheet. Bake at 400 degrees F for about 10 minutes until cookies are light brown on top. Remove to rack and cool.

Yield: 15 to 18 cookies.

menu

Cakes & Desserts

Pineapple Tarts
Cake Cones
Pulitzer Pudding Cake

Quick and Easy Apple Bundt
Cake
Fruit Cocktail Dessert
Pineapple Turnovers

Cakes & Desserts

Pineapple Tarts

1 (8 oz.) cream cheese

1 cup butter

2 cups flour

Pineapple preserves

Preheat oven to 400 degrees F.

Blend the cream cheese, butter and flour together. Roll pastry as thin as possible. Cut into 3 inch squares. Place a small amount of preserves in the center of each piece. Form a triangle and press edges together to seal. Bake at 400 degrees F until golden color, about 10 minutes.

Cake Cones

6 flat-bottomed ice cream cones

Whipped frosting

Muffin or cake mix batter

Spoon about 2 tablespoons of prepared muffin or cake mix batter into flat-bottomed ice cream cones. Microwave on High 20 to 40 seconds. or until cake is light and springy to the touch. Some moist spots may remain, but will dry upon standing.

Cool on wire rack. Let stand 3 minutes. Top with prepared whipped topping, frosting or scoop of ice cream, if desired.

Yield: 6 cupcake cones.

Pulitzer Pudding Cake

1 (21 oz.) can cherry pie filling

1 layer size box cake mix (or use 1/2 of a regular cake mix box)

1 cup nuts, chopped

1/2 cup butter

Preheat oven to 350 degrees F.

Pour the cherry pie filling in a 9 inch pie pan. Sprinkle the dry cake mix evenly over the pie filling. Sprinkle with nuts. Dot with small pieces of butter. Bake at 350 degrees F for 45 minutes.

Quick and Easy Apple Bundt Cake

1 (15.25 oz.) box spice cake mix

1 (21 oz.) can apple pie filling

2 teaspoons vegetable oil

2 eggs

Preheat oven to 350 degrees F.

Combine pie filling, oil and eggs. Add cake mix and stir until well combined. Pour into oiled and floured Bundt pan. Bake at 350 degrees F for 50 minutes.

Fruit Cocktail Dessert

1 (3.4 oz.) package instant vanilla pudding mix

1 (15 oz.) can fruit cocktail, undrained

1/2 cup miniature marshmallows

Chopped pecans

In a bowl, combine pudding mix and fruit cocktail; mix well. Fold in marshmallows and pecans just before serving. Keep refrigerated.

Yield: 6 servings.

Pineapple Turnovers

1 cup butter, softened

1 (8 oz.) cream cheese, softened

2 cups flour

1 (21 oz.) can pineapple pie filling

Preheat oven to 350 degrees F.

Combine butter, cream cheese and flour in bowl; mix well. Chill overnight. Roll dough 1/8 inch thick on lightly floured surface. Cut into 6" rounds. Place 1 tablespoon pie filling on each round. Fold pastry over. Moisten edges with small amount of water; seal. Prick tops with fork. Place on baking sheet. Bake at 350 degrees F for 30 minutes.

Yield: 2 dozen.

Other Books by Bonnie Scott

IN JARS SERIES – InJars.com

100 Easy Recipes in Jars
100 More Easy Recipes in Jars
Desserts in Jars

CAMPING – CampingFreebies.com

100 Easy Camping Recipes
Camping Recipes: Foil Packet Cooking

Bacon Cookbook: 150 Easy Bacon Recipes
Slow Cooker Comfort Foods
150 Easy Classic Chicken Recipes
Grill It! 125 Easy Recipes
Soups, Sandwiches and Wraps
Simply Fleece

Fish & Game Cookbook
Cookie Indulgence: 150 Easy Cookie Recipes
Pies and Mini Pies
Holiday Recipes: 150 Easy Recipes and Gifts From Your Kitchen

All titles available in Paperback and Kindle versions at Amazon.com

Printed in Great Britain
by Amazon